5 Things Schools Don't Teach

How You Can Create Educational Success for Your Children

© 2019 Adia Wilson, M.A. All rights reserved.

ISBN 978-0-359-74347-6

Foreword

Growing up, my late grandmother often shared vivid stories of her upbringing in South Carolina. Just two generations out of slavery, she and her 10 siblings managed to prosper during Jim Crow, when discrimination and segregation were law. Tardiness, cleanliness, politeness, education and the development of a skillset were common themes in these fascinating stories.

To my grandmother and her siblings, education was seen as an invaluable tool that could increase their opportunities to thrive and improve their quality of life. Despite this belief, my grandmother's stories also described a clear educational apartheid that still resonates today.

My own experience as a student in the New York City public-school system was amazing, though far from perfect. Classrooms were typically filled with over 25 students and at times, there were hardly enough chairs or textbooks to suffice. The support services that were available seemed to provide little aid to students and families who desperately needed to build better lives.

While my mother would have preferred to put me in private school, having access to some of the world's greatest institutions and resources offered an abundance of dynamic learning opportunities and exposures. Studying the performing arts provided me with outlets to express myself and build skills and confidence. In particular, dance kept me occupied and disciplined in the 'concrete jungle'. Sadly, many of my peers who could have benefited from receiving more support, continue to exist in a cycle of ignorance, poverty, and incarceration.

At Howard University, my experience differed drastically from what I encountered in the nation's largest public-school system. An all-Black institution, Howard had a legacy of attracting and nurturing highly-successful individuals. I took the opportunity to learn among an international body of scholars who were ambitious, confident, refined and talented. Completely inspired by this phenomenal journey, I began to ponder, *"What opportunities were provided to Howard students that may not have been provided to others? Did our families value education more? Were we given better support and guidance?"*

After graduating, I unknowingly began a career as an educator and administrator. My longtime compassion for youth led me to a part-time position as a tutor as I continued my search for full-time work. Over time, I honed invaluable instructional and managerial skills. Through my work with several non-profit and educational organizations, I learned to write and deliver engaging arts and academic curricula and manage contracts, programs and budgets. At the same time, I began to discover the multifaceted issues that plague urban communities and education.

Despite my commitment to creating change in the American educational landscape, I often felt defeated. My desire to gain a deeper understanding of the social, cultural, political and economic factors that affect an individual's educational attainment led me to graduate studies. The research I conducted presented mounting evidence that schooling alone does not improve social inequalities. *5 Things Schools Don't Teach* was created to offer guidance on how we can enrich education in underserved communities and increase chances of academic and personal success in underserved youth.

Most parents recognize that doing well in school can help children succeed later in life, yet an overwhelming number lack information on the educational process. Learning how to prepare children for schooling, how best to develop their talent, and where to find support are the keys to educational success. I believe that those who are reading this book share the same desire to improve our society through the education of our children.

Schools or other educational institutions do not provide this valuable information in an outright way. My goal is to allow parents to discover practices that can better direct and shape their experience. It is my pleasure to contribute to the upward mobility of *all* children and communities by increasing access to knowledge and resources. Thank you for allowing me to share!

*I dedicate this book to my late grandmother
Nannie Wilson.*

TABLE OF CONTENTS

Introduction.....................**1**

I: Education Begins Before Children Enter Schooling..........................**8**

II: Summer Break = Summer Learning..........**17**

III: Building Strong, Positive Connections between Home and School............**25**

IV: Building Capital through Socialization......**33**

V: Expectations Create Situations......**42**

Reflection....................................**50**

Introduction

Education gives students the opportunity to excel both in school and life, yet there are many factors that prevent schools from closing the achievement gap. First, many low-income children face vast inequalities *before* they even enter school. Once inside, they are typically placed in low-resource schools as early as kindergarten. Schools located in low-income communities are often underfunded, and have a hard time attracting and keeping quality teachers. They also face great difficulties in addressing students' needs.

According to a 2017 U.S. Department of Education report, Blacks and Hispanics continue to rank last in terms of graduation rates, college attendance and the labor market. While we should expect schools to increase academic achievement for all students, regardless of race or class, it is virtually impossible for them to eliminate all major pre-existing social inequalities.

Educational, occupational, and financial resources vary drastically among families. This is why *all* parents must become equipped with the knowledge and tools needed to create the educational success that their children deserve. Understanding various aspects of educational development and discovering practices that benefit children inside the school setting can place them at a great advantage. Sure, educating a child can be a daunting task, but the best results are produced through organization and planning.

Before we begin, let's create a framework by comparing the educational journey to a marathon. Say it's your first marathon. What steps would you take to prepare for it? First of all, you're most likely thinking, "*Where do I even begin*?!" One great way to prepare is to study the course prior to the event. This way, there will be no surprises when you actually run the race. Ample mental preparation can also help to instill confidence and discipline before and during the race.

What's my point here? Not only do you have to plan and prepare to complete this great course of action, but much of this work would take place *prior to*, or *outside of* the actual marathon. Knowing what you're getting into, establishing a routine, (including fueling the runner's body and mind properly) and even building a support system would increase your chances of success. Similarly, attending school is only a fraction of the educational development process. What happens *outside* the classroom matters tremendously.

While each individual has varying abilities and circumstances, showing up prepared to perform to the best of one's ability makes all the difference. As we move through each of the following five sections, let's continue to view education in the same way: as a marathon. Got it? Great! Now let's get to it!

You can't start running right out of the gate without having a plan that helps you gradually build up your endurance. Creating a training schedule will help prepare the runner both physically and mentally for the demands he or she will face during the marathon.

1. Education Begins Before Children Enter Schooling

Numerous studies have explored the differences in academic performance among young children at the point of school entry. What they've found is that vast differences in cognitive skills performance exist *before* children arrive in kindergarten. Furthermore, it is how parents read and converse at home with their children that create these differences.

Cognitive skills include information processing, memory, decision making, problem solving and language learning. Children who score at the lowest levels on cognitive skills tests when they arrive in kindergarten are consequently placed into lower ability groups. This placement is a major contributor to the academic achievement gap, which only widens as they continue through school.

While family structure and educational expectations play a significant role, it is the amount of *language experience* a child receives that accounts for more of the distinct variation in scores. One groundbreaking study observed the average amount of language experience young American children receive per hour from their parents, and the data revealed huge contrasts in the amount of interaction between parents and children.

The number of words addressed to children differed across income groups. In a typical hour, children from families on welfare were provided half as much experience as children from working-class families, and less than a third of the experience given to children from high income families (600, 1,200 and 2,100 words, respectively). In other words, children from better financial circumstances had far more language exposure to draw from.

These results alone illustrate how important language experience is to a child's cognitive development, but the study also highlighted *'extra talk',* as another major contributor to the vast differences in cognitive performance. The 'extra talk' exhibited by some families and parents involved more diverse vocabulary, complex ideas, subtle guidance and affirmative feedback.

Extra talk is especially significant because it allows children to stretch themselves cognitively. When children are assisted by an older individual (a parent, baby-sitter, teacher or sibling), they can complete more difficult tasks.

As parents engage maturing children in more complex activities, the complexity of what is said will increase without planning. Furthermore, when that older person models a behavior, provides instruction and offers encouragement, kids also use that as a guide for their own performance. This increases their ability to work independently in preparation for schooling.

In addition to increasing a child's vocabulary by expanding the number of topics through 'extra talk', *the amount of time* parents spend conversing with their children makes a great difference. All of the families observed talked mostly about whatever they happened to be doing at the moment, yet few parents spent twice as much time interacting with their children.

Lastly, the amount of language experience parents provide their children *before age three* is most influential because this is when cognitive development is most rapid. As a result, the period from 0 to 3 years of age is when the inequality gap first emerges. This gap in vocabulary knowledge reaches a peak during the preschool phase and remains constant thereafter.

While attending school reduces pre-existing cognitive gaps, schools are not equalizing in an absolute sense. This means that, to an extent, the inequality we see in cognitive performance when children enter kindergarten is attributable to differences in family practices. The amount of talk that occurs within your family not only sets the initial course of accumulating language experience, but also has a great influence on the years to follow.

Parents should draw their children into adult conversation once they become verbal, so their children can practice expressing their own thoughts and opinions. Elaborating talk beyond an exchange of necessary instruction such as by sharing ideas, prepares children to solidify social relationships outside the home. Get your children ahead of the game and set them on a course that creates positive, permanent results. Just create your 'training' schedule, talk and play! On to number two!

So, you've got your plan together and you've built up your endurance. To keep the runner physically and mentally prepared, the training schedule must remain consistent. If not, they will lose ground as they progress throughout the marathon.

2. Summer Break = Summer Learning

Children begin formal schooling with different skill levels, partly because they are exposed to different home environments and neighborhoods. Not only do most children spend the majority of their time outside of school, but the quality of their non-school environments varies drastically.

Attendance in kindergarten and school have somewhat of an equalizing effect as children from all backgrounds are exposed to peer and teacher interaction. Once children enter school, they gain cognitive skills at approximately the same rate. Then, gaps in reading and math skills grow primarily during the summer, which suggests that non-school factors are highly influential.

Since schooling occurs in some seasons and not others, the rate of children's cognitive development reflects the schoolyear calendar. Learning during the schoolyear is a product of both school and non-school factors while summer learning reflects only the influence of non-school factors.

Unlike formal schooling, summer break has no mandatory structure, leaving parents fully responsible for structuring all of their children's time. This time might consist of limited stimulation, leaving children to entertain themselves, or it might consist of an arrangement of activities that occupy the entire summer. In addition, children are not limited to developing the skills outlined in their school curriculum. The summer can be utilized to pursue their own interests and develop their talents.

Families from various backgrounds construct childcare and activities for their children during summer vacation in different ways. To maximize summer learning, construct a child's time by combining activities. In addition to day camps and family vacations, fill schedules with organized lessons and other educational enrichment activities. Choosing a summer camp or program that matches a child's needs and interests enhances his or her development.

Financial resources and parents' time should not stop them from seeking information on affordable and free programs that coincide with parents' rigid work schedules. Researching prices for camp, using social connections to obtain discounts or driving to less expensive locations is a worthy investment.

Information and activities are also now more directly accessible to children. Depending on their age, they can travel to schools, community centers, libraries, parks and recreation centers. Why not have them share the responsibility and be a part of the decision-making and planning? Furthermore, spaces like these provide opportunities for children and parents alike to create, build and utilize their own social networks. Networks lead to *opportunity*.

There are endless ways to provide learning experiences for kids, both outside of school and at home. As a teen in Harlem, I remember seeing children play outside all day during the summer. There were tons of summer camps available for even the poorest children, and it seemed unfair that no one had considered enrolling them in a program. An entire world was awaiting their discovery, even at the local museum or library.

Young, growing minds need to be constantly engaged. 'Free time' should always be specified and limited. The bottom line is, while some children are spending their days relaxing, playing outside, or sitting in front of the television, the children who are learning during the summer are continuing to make significant cognitive gains.

Parents who want to mold well-rounded, competitive kids must view the summer season as an extension of formal education. Keep up the momentum and be intentional about how you construct your child's time *all* year round.

When time is supervised and organized, children will thrive off of that structure. This leads me to number three!

For any marathon runner, finishing the race is a major accomplishment, but focus more on building a positive experience, rather than trying to run too hard. Get support and encouragement from friends and family to help boost morale and stay focused on the goal.

3. Building Strong, Positive Connections between Home and School

The inconsistencies between practices at home and school bring to light a dilemma many parents face across the country: while teaching their kids that success in school translates into success later in life, children and families often resent school and view it as a threat to their own values. Creating a home culture that values education, however, is most critical to academic success.

Finding ways to establish a relationship between home and school will vary for each family. The foundation of this relationship, however, is interconnection, where education is viewed as a *shared responsibility* between teachers and parents. By leaving schooling primarily to the school, some families might feel they are avoiding added stress. While many teachers are trusted professionals who have their students' best interests in mind, extrinsic indicators, such as grades, stickers and written comments, aren't enough to track how kids are achieving in school.

Teachers typically aim to be positive, and parents may not always recognize when a child is falling behind. Once a student is behind, it becomes difficult to catch up. Parents who build strong interconnections between home and school are more likely to identify if (and when) challenges occur. They also have a greater ability to access resources to shape their children's school experience.

This connection between family and school also yields multiple benefits. Having extensive information on your children's schooling, including the curriculum or the educational process, gives your kids a *competitive advantage*. Parents can also find ways to reinforce the curriculum at home and during the summer, as discussed earlier.

Creating a strong network of social relationships for yourself also provides a strong foundation for parent involvement in schooling. When parents form close ties with other parents whose children attend the same school, they can obtain more information about the specifics of their child's school experience. Use what you know to request special school programs or specific teachers.

Through the networks you build, you'll also unlock information on supplemental services, (such as tutoring or counseling) if you feel your child needs additional support. Last but certainly not least, your network can exist as a solid support system. Sharing ideas, best practices or even childcare responsibilities makes parental involvement more effective and efficient. I am a firm believer that it takes a village to raise a child. If necessary, involve an older sibling, grandparent, godparent or neighbor. No matter what a family's circumstances, parental (extended family, or community) involvement is a *must*. I certainly owe much of my success to the 'village' that raised me.

Like school, the home is an institution, and the earlier you establish connections between the two, the better. Though children become more independent as they grow, the need for family involvement remains constant. As kids approach adolescence, setting standards and expectations is a huge part in maintaining this connection. We'll discuss this later, but for now, on to part four!

The mindset and confidence you establish during training can have a positive influence on your attitude and performance during the race. A great way to train mentally is to immerse the runner in a number of training activities that will develop multiple skills. This way, they build confidence and discipline, which are essential components of mental preparation.

4. Building Capital through Socialization

By definition, capital is any source of profit, advantage or power, an asset or assets. Humans too, possess capital and it includes our collective skills, knowledge, talents, abilities, experience, intelligence, training, judgment and wisdom. These intangible assets are then utilized to create *economic value* for individuals, employers and communities at large.

French authors Pierre Bourdieu and Jean-Claude Passeron introduced the concept of *'cultural capital'* to the world to explain differences in academic performance and achievement among schoolchildren. They defined it as a person's education, knowledge and intellectual skills that provide an advantage in achieving a higher social status in society.

Specifically, cultural capital refers to an individual's *social assets*: one's education, style of dress and speech.

Socialization is a process that starts at home during childhood when kids acquire language styles and cultural tastes. Through interaction and experience, socialization cultivates children's cognitive and social skills. By gaining more exposure to adults through various activities (academic, arts and sports) children learn to interact with authority figures in ways that benefit them later in school and adulthood. Building extensive experience with adults, trains children to advocate for themselves as they learn to negotiate with others.

Exposure to non academic activities can offer positive, healthy influences and opportunities. Additionally, the values and attitudes students encounter among their social circle is highly influential. Once students enter high school, differences in achievement derive heavily from differences in peer environment.

To many, taking on an after-school job or participating in extracurricular activities is seen as a sign of diligence and the best way to build character. To get your student across the finish line (to graduation), there are some things you should consider. Here are some reasons why being involved in outside activities and how long is significant:

Students who are involved in extracurricular activities are more likely to perform better. School-sponsored extracurricular activities can strengthen students' commitment to school. By helping students develop an emotional attachment to the institution and teachers, this bond has the potential to spill over into the academic domain.

Working or being involved in extracurricular activities for more than 20 hours per week is likely to be harmful; whereas, 10 or less hours does not appear to take a constant toll on school performance. Participating in high-level commitment sports like football or basketball, can at times, have a negative impact on academic achievement. In high school, for example, many student athletes are expected to practice both before *and* after school, in addition to the actual games. This leaves many students too tired to devote sufficient time and concentration to their studies. This does not discount the fact that participating in major team sports may actually enhance the achievement of struggling students, particularly those who might otherwise disengage from school.

Similar to summer learning, cultural capital is considered both valuable and necessary to a child's development. Through time invested at dance studios and swimming lessons, for example, children build confidence, learn discipline and how to present themselves in various settings. Academic success is only *partly* about school work. Socializing children helps them master the cognitive skills required to perform well in school and beyond.

I encourage parents to think of their children as assets that accrue value over time through *socialization.* When people develop multiple skills, a vast array of knowledge and a growing network, more options become available to them. In a world that's becoming increasingly competitive and technological, developing a strong, diverse skillset means young people can create multiple options for themselves as well. The greatest benefit of accruing cultural capital is the positive sense of self-worth children gain. Number five makes *all* of this possible. Ready to bring it on home? Let's go!

Some parts of the race will prove more challenging than others. Every race will unfold differently due to the terrain, weather and the conditioning of the runner. When someone is well prepared for a marathon, that person's muscles have the capacity to push into unknown territory.

5. Expectations Create Situations

Unfortunately, expectations and sometimes labels, are placed on children as soon as they enter kindergarten and may set them on a course of action that could affect the rest of their lives. Self-fulfilling prophecy is activated in the classroom the same way it is in everyday life and plays a huge role in educational outcomes.

While expectations aren't always guaranteed to be self-fulfilling, in many cases, what we expect about people triggers us to treat them in a way that makes them respond according to expectations and the cycle continues. At times, others provide feedback that isn't necessarily true, but we've convinced ourselves it is. This helps to reinforce the original belief.

Social scientist Ray Rist helped shed light on labeling practices when he examined the relationship between social-class and academic achievement. While observing a teacher place students in separate learning groups, he noticed that the teacher determined placement based on external factors, such as dress and speech. One group of students made up the group of 'fast learners', while the other two groups were labeled 'slow learners'. This was determined by the eighth day of kindergarten. Not one formal evaluation of the children had taken place.

From the data he gathered, Rist determined that the children who were randomly selected as 'fast learners' somehow caused teachers to treat them differently, with the result being that the children *actually did* perform better by the end of the year.

Teachers have the authority to claim almost exclusively, whether or not mastery of content has occurred. Moreover, they provide authorization for promotion to the next grade. The labels and expectations given to children by schools and society in general make it necessary for families and communities at large to take responsibility for setting the standards and determining the accuracy of these expectations and labels.

When parents leave it up to others to place value and standards on their children, they will be the ones determining their children's academic ability. As their *first* teachers, set those labels and standards before your children arrive to school. Consider teaching your child confidence in his or her abilities as a part of school readiness. Implementing a positive self-fulfilling prophecy that is characterized by positive feedback, compliments and affirmations can have such a deep, positive impact on a child's academic performance.

Imagine what results you could create if you intentionally labeled and believed your children to be intelligent and gifted. What if you expected your kids to do well in school, to always try their best, and to take pride in their work? Envision a household where you treated your children like scholars, and the standard was regularly discussing their wins and challenges around schooling. This positive outlook, matched by these constructive practices, can actually help parents create and direct their children's schooling experience!

When parents view education as an investment and establish a home culture that values it, children are much more likely to uphold the expectations and standards required of them. Facing challenges at school is an inevitable part of the process but setting a positive tone for your kids' educational journey provides them with a healthy foundation. Consistently offering encouragement, patiently listening and asking challenging questions will help you better understand and meet their needs. Most of all, staying informed by monitoring their activities and progress will be the key to creating solutions and knowing what adjustments to make.

Running a marathon isn't easy, but it sure as hell is rewarding. Indeed, it is an extreme journey that demands resilience, determination, willpower and focus. Congratulations, you've crossed the finish line!

Reflection

Educating children does not come with instructions and every family's needs, preferences and abilities differ drastically. While this book does not offer guidance on the best schools or what works best for whom, it does provide a framework for *educational planning.* Parents' resources vary greatly but like school, the home is an institution, and it is left to *you* to do the work necessary to prepare your children for successful lives.

Though the schools must change and continue to be held accountable, the fact remains: what children do outside the classroom has a great influence on how they perform inside. Sitting in a classroom all day means very little when students aren't equipped with the tools or skills required to thrive beyond school, let alone graduate. The fact that cognitive growth is more rapid early in life than later, underlines the significance of very early education; specifically, the need for language-related and school readiness instruction. If you want to build children who are competitive, articulate and thoughtful, start at *home* and *early*.

Pre-school, after-school activities and summer learning boost both academic *and* personal growth. Extracurricular activities expose children to ideas, people and places they might not otherwise experience in their immediate home, neighborhood or school environments. When students devote a great deal of time to an extracurricular activity, they spend much of their free time in the company of peers who share that interest. The circle of friends a child chooses might make all the difference between mediocre and excellent school performance.

Education is not just about earning good grades, participating in extracurricular activities and graduating with plans to go to college. What it really provides students with is the ability to move beyond their current socio-economic status as they become well-rounded, adaptable and skillful. More than anything, education prepares young people for the opportunities which arise to enhance their talents. As the great American educator and activist Marian Wright Edelman once stated, education as a value "is sustained by the belief that freedom and education go hand in hand, that learning and training are essential to economic quality and independence."

It was my absolute pleasure to share these five practices with you. My hope is that in some respect, I've increased your understanding on educational development. I encourage you to revisit this book at any time, as you create your own unique educational journey for your family. Be organized, be intentional and stay committed to their success. Get your runner across that finish line! I believe in you!

Cheers to the little ones who hold the keys to the future. May they be the change we need in this world, as they add value to their families, communities and the world at large.

www.ingramcontent.com/pod-product-compliance
Lightning Source LLC
Chambersburg PA
CBHW060504110426
42738CB00055B/2613